D1135040

Card Games

Terry Eagle

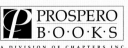

PROSPERO
B·O·O·K·S
A DIVISION OF CHAPTERS INC.

This edition produced for Prospero Books,
a division of Chapters, Inc., in 2000
by arrangement with Mars Publishing

M 10 9 8 7 6 5 4 3 2 1

ISBN: 1-55267-080-5

This is a MARS book

Edited, designed and produced by Haldane Mason, London

Art Director: Ron Samuels
Editorial Director: Sydney Francis
Editor: Jane Ellis
Design: Sarah Collins

Manufactured in China

Contents

Introduction

**Welcome to the exciting world of card games! This book will give you
clear instructions on how to play over 20 of the world's most popular
games, ranging from simple forms of Patience to the complex game of
Bridge, which requires four people to play. In each section the games
gradually become more complex. Happy playing!**

Each game is explained
in the same sequence.
Firstly, the aim of the
game is given. Then the
method of play is set
out, followed by any
useful notes or hints.
For some games, variant
forms are also given,
which are usually
slightly more difficult.

The pack

A standard pack has 52
cards, divided into four
suits of 13 cards each.
Each suit is clearly
marked by its own
symbol – hearts, clubs,
diamonds and spades.
Each card has a value.
Aces can either be top
(high) or bottom (low),
depending on the game.
Then, in descending
order, it is king, queen,
jack, and the number
cards from 10 to 2. In
some games two extra
cards, the jokers, are

also used. You can
usually assign any value
to these cards.

Shuffling and cutting

At the start of every
game, unless the rules
say otherwise, the pack
is shuffled, so that the
cards are thoroughly
mixed; and then cut. To
cut the pack after it has
been shuffled, get
another player to lift
around half of the
shuffled pack, and place
that half underneath, so
that the upper half of
the pack becomes the
lower half.

Rules

Many card games have
developed over a long
period, which means
that the same games
can be played with
slightly different rules.
It is extremely
important, especially

with gambling games,
that the rules are agreed
at the beginning and
that all the players
follow them.

Cutting and drawing
for dealer

A dealer is chosen by
cutting or drawing: each
player in turn cuts the
pack or draws a card
from it. The highest card
usually wins, but in
some games it is the
lowest. If there is a tie,
the players involved
repeat the cut or draw.

Gambling

Many card games can be
used for gambling.
Betting can take many
forms: it doesn't have to
be money. Currency can
be anything from plastic
chips to actual cash.
There is one basic safety
rule – never bet what
you haven't got.

Introduction

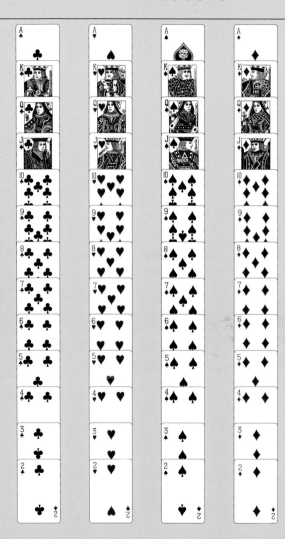

Patience Games

Patience is a game for one person and there are many different variations. In these games, your aim is to beat the cards. It is immensely satisfying when you do. And of course if you cheat, the only person you're cheating is you! You need a large table to lay out the cards, although it is possible to get smaller-sized packs of cards for Patience.

Aces Up

Aim of game
To be left with only the four aces.

Method of play
Use the standard 52-card pack. Cards rank in descending order from ace to 2. Deal four cards in a row, face up. If two or more cards of the same suit are dealt, discard the lower-value one(s), leaving a space. Deal a further four cards face up on top of the first ones, including the space(s). Again discard the lower cards of a duplicated suit. An eliminated card may uncover another that can also be eliminated. Once six deals have been made, you can move the top card or cards of any pile into a space, before the next deal. Continue this process until all the cards are discarded and you finish with a row of four aces.

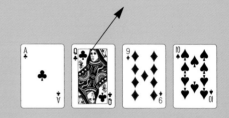

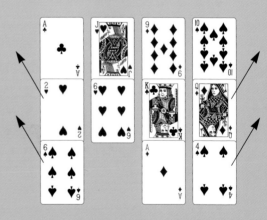

Arrows show that these cards will be discarded from the layout.

Note
If a discard is at the top of a pile, only the top card is discarded.

Beleaguered Castle

Aim of game
To build up four piles in suit and sequence, ace (low) to king.

Method of play
Use the standard 52-card pack. Arrange the four aces in a column (not overlapping) to form your foundation pile. The tableau is made by dealing six cards to each side of the aces, alternately left and right, in overlapping rows. Only the outer card of each row is available. These can be placed on the foundation pile if they form the next card in suit and sequence.

Alternatively, they can be placed at the outer end of another row, but only in sequence of descending pip value; the suit does not matter, e.g. place a 5 of hearts on a 6 of spades. If a row is empty, any available card may be placed in it. In this way cards or sequences can be moved around, but this is still a tricky game to complete.

The arrows indicate how cards could be moved.

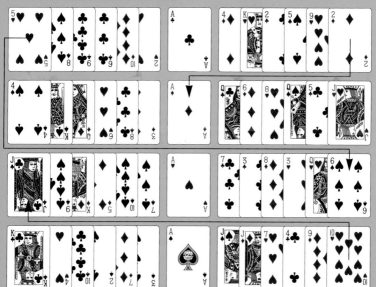

9

Castles in Spain

Aim of game
To build up suits, in sequence, from the foundation cards.

Method of play

Use the standard 52-card pack. Deal a row of five cards, laying them face down from left to right. Above this row lay a row of four cards, then a row of three above that. Finally, place one card above the centre card of the row of three. Then lay down two further sets, also face down, on top of the first set.

You now have 13 cards left. Lay them face up, one by one, on top of the existing piles, keeping to the pattern. This makes 13 depot piles. Any aces showing are played to the foundation row, once the tableau is set out. The card beneath the ace is turned up and becomes available for play. Available cards may be played either on to their foundation pile, or in descending sequence of alternate colour on another depot pile.

Sequences or part sequences may be moved from one depot pile to another or to fill any spaces that are created. The cards cannot be redealt.

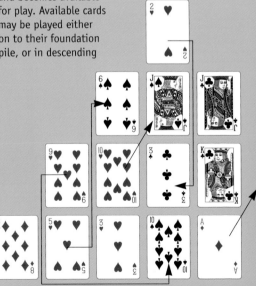

The arrows indicate how cards could be moved after layout.

To foundation row

Flower Garden

Aim of game
To build up each suit in ascending sequence from its ace (low ace).

Method of play
Use the standard 52-card pack and deal 36 cards, face up, in six overlapping columns of six. This is your garden. The bottom card of each column is available for play.

Deal the remaining 16 cards in a face-up row. This is your bouquet, and all cards in it are available at any time.

As aces become available, place them in a row above the layout, face up, and build up on them from 2 to king in each suit.

You can create four auxiliary columns in which cards may be placed in descending order of suit, with available cards being played to the bottom of the columns. When a column is used up, any available card can be used to start a new one.

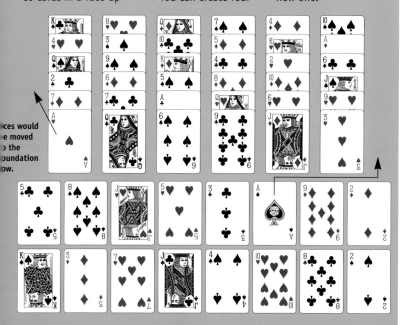

ces would
e moved
o the
oundation
ow.

11

Frustration

Aim of game
**Build eight columns of the same suits rising from ace (low)
or descending from king to ace.**

Method of play

Use two standard packs of cards. Shuffle them into one, and deal a row of 11 cards, face up. Take out any kings or aces, and set these out as a foundation row.

Add any cards that go consecutively in the same suit (e.g. queen beneath king; 2 over ace). Fill any gaps in the row from the pack. Once no more moves are possible, deal a second row of 11 cards under the top one. From this point, no card can be played to the foundation unless it is the next card in its sequence – played straight to the foundation; or if it is the only card in a column. If you lay it in the tableau you must leave it there. This rule goes on until all cards have been dealt. After

that, all cards at the foot of a column are available for adding to the foundation rows.

Within the tableau, you can add cards of the same suit in either ascending or descending order. If the bottom card is a 9 of diamonds, you can add an 8 to it, and than either a 9 or a 7 to the 8. When you

have exhausted all possible moves, pick up all the remaining cards from the layout, starting with the left-hand column and then the other columns in sequence, and lay them out again, one row of 11 at a time. You can redeal the cards twice in this way.

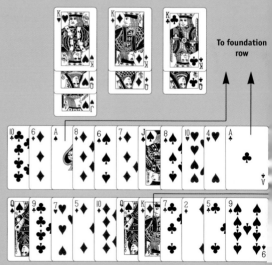

To foundation row

To foundation row

Lucas

Aim of game
To build up eight columns in sequence from aces (low) to kings.

Method of play
Use two standard packs. Take out the eight aces from the two packs and arrange them in a row as bases, with aces of the same suit side by side.

Shuffle the packs together and deal 13 columns of three cards each, face up, below the bases. Only the lowest row is available. You can build upwards on the bases, by suits, and downwards on the columns, by suit. Once

you have moved all the cards out of a column, you can move another available card, preferably of high value, into the space to restart the column. When you can no longer move cards in the layout, deal another card from the pack, face up. If you deal a card that cannot be used (because it cannot be placed into any sequence), place it face up in a discard pile. The top card of the

discard pile is always available for play.

Variant
Big Forty. In this form you shuffle the entire packs, including the aces, and deal ten columns of four cards each. The rules are then as in Lucas. As aces become available, set them out above the layout as bases for building columns.

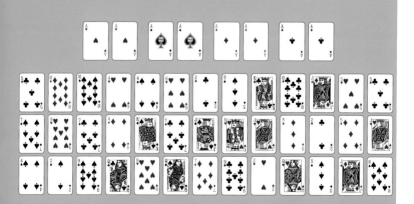

Miss Milligan

Aim of game
Build eight columns of the same suits in ascending sequence, aces (low) to kings.

Method of play
Use two standard packs. Shuffle and deal eight cards in a row, face up. Remove any aces and place them above the row, as bases. Replace with another card dealt from the pack. From the layout, take cards that can be built upwards

from the aces. Within the layout, you can arrange cards in descending sequence of alternate colour. When all possible moves have been made, deal a second set of eight cards, each one overlapping a card in the first row, or filling

a gap in that row. Now only the second eight cards are available to play, but when any of them have been moved, you may move the card that was underneath.

When no more moves are possible, deal a third set of eight in the same way, overlapping

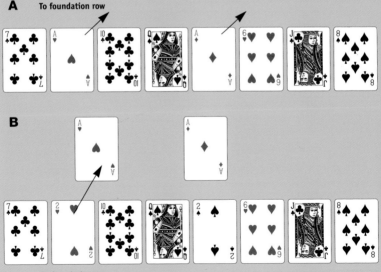

A   To foundation row

B

To foundation row

14

Miss Milligan

the second row or filling gaps. This goes on until you have completed 13 deals and all cards are in play. Now you continue to build your columns. But at this point you are not restricted to the last-dealt cards. You can 'waive' a card at the foot of any layout column, by removing it to one side, and playing the card that is thus released. The waived card remains available, and once it is played, you can waive another.

Variant

Some players waive whole sequences from the layout column, to be played back card by card.

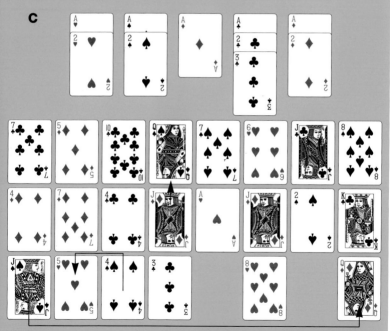

Your layout will start to look something like this after three or four rows have been dealt. Arrows show the start of descending columns.

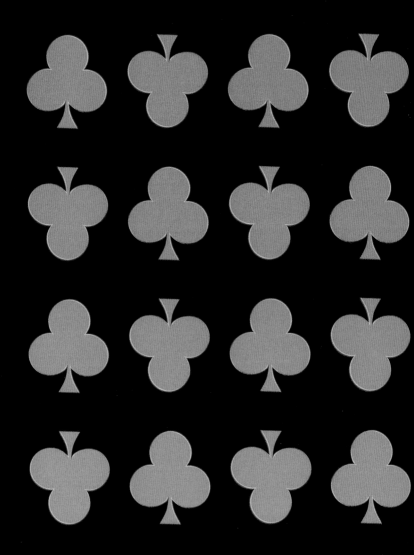

Games for Two or More Players

Many card games can be played by different numbers of people. Games such as Pontoon (page 22) can be played by two to eight people. Most games have an ideal number of players, which suits the game best.

Pinochle

There is a whole range of Pinochle games. It began as a two-hander (two players), but some variants can be played by up to five players. The game here is two-handed Pinochle.

Aim of game
By scoring maximum points through winning key tricks and making melds.

Scoring values of individual cards

Ace	11
Ten	10
King	4
Queen	3
Jack	2
Nine of trumps	10
Other nines	0

Method of play

Use two standard packs. You need to form a 48-card pack, by combining the packs and removing all cards with a pip value of between 2 and 8.

The range is ace (high) to 9. Before play, players agree on the winning score. This is usually 1,000 but it can be 1,500. Cut for dealer. Each player is dealt 12 cards in three packets of four. The next card is turned face up and

denotes trumps. The pack is laid face down across the trump card. If the card is a 9 (9 of trumps is known as a dix), the dealer awards himself 10 points.

The non-dealer leads, and the dealer can follow with any card. The trick is won by the highest card of the lead suit, or by a trump. If both players put down identical cards, the first one down takes the trick. The winner of the

trick may lay down his melds, face up, but can score only for one meld per trick. He then draws the first card from the top of the pack to add to his hand; his opponent does likewise.

Before leading, a player may lay selected cards from his hand on the table, face up. This is known as melding. Melds are combinations of cards with a special value (see opposite and page 21).

Pinochle

Meld names and values

Meld scores are noted immediately, as the cards remain in play.

Ace, ten, king, queen, jack of trump suit 150

Four aces (no pairs) 100

Four kings (no pairs) 80

Four queens (no pairs) 60

Four jacks (no pairs) 40

Pinochle

A player can set down more than one meld at a time, but he can only claim points for one single meld for each trick played. A card used in one kind of meld may be used later to form a different type of meld. Thus a player could meld four kings (each of a different suit) for 80 points, then add the queen of diamonds to the king of diamonds for a royal marriage, or even a trump marriage, if diamonds are trumps. But if he turns up the other king of diamonds, he cannot marry him to the same queen; he would have to find a different type of meld. If he went on to turn up the queens of hearts, clubs and spades, he could use his queen of diamonds for a four-queen meld at 60 points. The winner of the trick leads to the next, either from his hand or from his meld. In making a new meld, the winner of a trick must use a fresh

card; he cannot just recombine existing melds.

Play goes on until the full pack has been drawn. The player who lost the twelfth trick picks up the trump card. From then on, the two hands are played out, and the non-leader must follow suit or trump, if he can. Some players adopt the rule that the non-leader must not only follow suit, but play a higher card from the led suit, if he has one – but this is optional. At the finish of each hand, the deal moves to the other player.

Scoring

As scoring must be noted throughout the game, you need to keep a careful running total. It is a good idea to note the content of the meld as well as the actual score, to avoid argument. At the finish of the hand, each player counts the value of his cards. The winner of the

final trick gets an additional ten points. The game goes on until one player claims to have reached 1,000 points. Play stops and his score is checked; if correct, he wins. If he has added up wrongly, he loses.

Optional special melds (see opposite) can be agreed between the players before the game.

Double Pinochle: A player holding a pair of queens of spades and a pair of jacks of diamonds may be allowed to meld them as a unit for 80 points, rather than treating them as two melds and picking up only 40 points each time. This helps to speed the game along.

Grand Pinochle: A player may combine a royal marriage of spades with a Pinochle as a single meld (king and queen of spades plus jack of diamonds) for 60 points; or 80 points if spades are trumps.

Pinochle

Trump marriage: king and queen of trumps 40

Royal marriage (king and queen of a non-trump suit) 20

Pinochle (queen of spades and jack of diamonds) 40

Dix (9 of the trump suit) 10

Optional special melds

Double Pinochle

Grand Pinochle

Pontoon

One of the most popular gambling games, known in the USA as Blackjack (see pages 46–47), and in France as Vingt-et-Un (Twenty-One). Plastic chips or matchsticks can be used instead of money.

Number of players
From two to eight or more.

Aim of game
To win stakes from the bank by getting a Pontoon or forming a hand which beats the banker's.

Scoring values

Players can choose whether aces are 1 or 11; kings, queens, jacks and 10s count as 10 points; other cards are worth the same as their pip value.

Method of play

Use the standard 52-card pack (two packs shuffled together for eight or more players). Cut the cards; the player with the highest card becomes both banker and dealer.

The banker deals one card to each player, starting on his left and ending with himself. His card remains face down; everyone else picks up their card. Starting from

the banker's left, the players place their initial bets (between agreed maximum and minimum levels). The banker then deals a second card to each player, and now all the players including the banker look at their two cards. If the banker has a Pontoon (ace – scoring at 11 – plus a 10), he lays it down, face up. Each player has to pay double their stake to the banker, and the round ends.

If the banker cannot declare a Pontoon, then each player, starting from his left, has an opportunity to acquire extra cards. A player with a Pontoon declares

it at this point by placing it on the table.

A player with two cards of equal value can split his hand, by laying the cards face up on the table and placing another stake equal to his first one. The banker deals another card, face down, to each of the two cards. If again there are equal-value cards, there can be a further split. Each hand may then be played, one after the other, during the player's turn.

Note: If the split cards are 10-point ones, they must be of the same nominal rank; two jacks may be split, but a jack and a king cannot.

Pontoon

Game 1: The banker pays out to the player with a Pontoon.

Banker

If a player's cards total under 21, he can say 'I'll buy one'. He must place another bet of at least the same amount as before, or up to double it, but not more. The banker then deals him another card face down. If his total is still under 21, he can buy again and increase his stake. This time he can raise it by any amount between the first bet and the second.

If the total is still under 21, he can buy and bet again, in the same way. If his total is under 21, a player can also say 'twist'. This means he receives another card face up, but does not increase the stake.

The player can then twist again if his total is low, until he has up to five cards, totalling under 21, in his hand. This forms a Five-Card Trick. A player can buy and then twist, but not twist and then buy.

A player may decide to 'stick' (not to take any extra cards). This is usual if his hand totals 15 or more. Play then passes to the next player on the left. If at any time a player's hand exceeds 21, he is 'bust', and must throw in his hand, face up, and lose his stake to the bank. A player who is bust on one split hand can continue to play the other hand.

Pontoon

Game 2: After the second round in this game, the banker has a Pontoon and each player has to pay double their stake to the banker.

Players who are dealt cards totalling 13 or 14 have the option to 'burn'. They hand their cards back to the dealer, who replaces them at the bottom of the pack and deals the player two new cards.

Burn

The banker has got a Pontoon.

When the players have completed their turns, the banker turns his two cards face up. He can then add up to three extra cards, or stay with his hand.

At the end of the round, after scoring is completed, there are several possibilities: if no one had a Pontoon,

the dealer adds all the used cards to the bottom of the pack and deals again, without shuffling. If there was a Pontoon, the cards are shuffled and cut before the next deal.

There is no change of banker unless he did not have a Pontoon, and another player did

have one, without splitting his hand. That player takes over the bank. If two or more players are eligible, then the one nearest the banker's left becomes the new banker. A banker can also sell the bank to another player, after any round.

Pontoon

Game 3: After four rounds, one player has gone bust; another has 'stuck' on 18; they will lose their bets to the banker another has reached a Five-Card Trick. The banker reached 19 so he pays out double to the Five-Card Trick.

Stuck on 18

Bust

Five-Card Trick

Banker

Scoring and paying

If the banker goes bust, he must pay the stake of each player who has not gone bust, with double to any player who has a Pontoon or a Five-Card Trick.

If the banker has 21 or less, with not more than four cards, he pays

stakes back to any player with a higher hand value, and collects from those with an equal or lower value.

A banker who stayed on 19 will say 'Paying 20'. All players then show their cards; those with hands of 21 or a Five-Card Trick receive double their stake.

A banker with 21 pays only to players with Pontoons and Five-Card Tricks.

If the banker has a Five-Card Trick, he pays only Pontoons (double the stake). Every other player, even those with Five-Card Tricks, have to pay double their stake to the banker.

Rummy

Number of players
Two to six.

Aim of game
To be the first player to 'go out' by getting rid of all cards.

Method of play
Use the standard 52-card pack. Aces are low. Cut for dealer (lowest card). Starting from the dealer's left, cards are dealt according to the number of players: ten each to two players; seven each to three or four; six each to five or more. Cards are dealt out singly in rotation. The rest of the pack is placed face down on the the table, and the top card is turned face up to start the discard pile.

A
Opening hands after deal

Rummy

Each player (starting on the dealer's left) draws a card from either the top of the pack (unseen) or from the discard pile. The object is to form melds of three or four, either by suit (consecutive, as 3-4-5-6 of clubs), or by value (as three kings). A player places his melds, if any, face down in front of him. He then discards a single card face up on the discard pile. This is the 'upcard'. Players can also add cards to the melds already laid down ('laying off').

A player does not have to lay down his melds; he can retain them and hope to go out in a single turn. This is known as to go rummy. The process continues until one player 'goes out' by melding, laying off, or discarding his last card. If the whole pack is exhausted and no one has gone out, the discard pile can be turned over, and the last upcard used to start a new discard pile.

Scoring

The player who goes out scores points for all the cards still held by his opponents: ten for each court card, 1 for each ace, and the other cards according to their pip value. A player who goes rummy gets double points.

Rummy can be, and often is, played as a gambling game, rather than simply to score points. Players should agree a value per point before play begins.

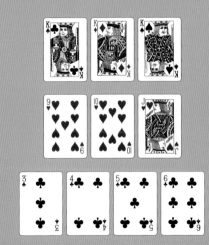

B

As the game progresses, players put down melds. Here are some examples.

27

Newmarket

This is a gambling game that involves betting on horses as you would at the races. Plastic chips or matchsticks can be used instead of money.

Number of players
Two to four.

Aim of game
To be the first player to go out by getting rid of all the cards, while collecting as many bets as you can along the way.

Method of play
Use two packs of cards. From one pack take four court cards, each of a different suit, e.g. jack of diamonds, queen of spades, king of hearts, ace of clubs. These are the 'horses' on which bets will be placed. Put them in the middle of the table and discard the rest of the pack. From the second pack remove and discard all cards with a pip value of 6 and under (aces are high). The remaining cards are all dealt out to the players, and a dummy hand is also dealt.

Betting
Players have to place their bets *before* looking at their cards. A player can bet as many chips or matchsticks on as many of the four horses as he likes, with a minimum of one. When more than one player bets on the same horse, there will only be one winner, so it is a good idea to make sure that every horse has at least one bet placed on it. Each player also has to pay one chip or matchstick into the 'kitty' as an entrance fee to the game.

Scoring
Now all players look at their cards. A good hand will hold at least one of the horse cards, and will also have a fairly even balance of black and red cards. All the players now have the option to buy the dummy hand, for the price of one matchstick into the kitty. The dealer has first refusal. If the dealer does not buy the dummy, then it is offered to the other players, starting with the player on his left, until it is bought and that player swaps his hand for the dummy. If no one buys the dummy it's a sure sign that everyone thinks they have a good hand. The player with the 7 of diamonds always starts the game, placing the card on the table in front of him and calling out 'seven of diamonds'. Then the player who

Newmarket

This is how the
cards are set up
before the start
of play.

1

The horse cards

3

2

Dummy hand

The kitty

Newmarket

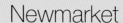

has the 8 of diamonds puts that card down in front of him, and calls out 'eight of diamonds'. Always build upwards in suit. Whenever a player puts down, he must always call it out. This helps to keep the game moving quickly. Remember that, because there is a dummy hand, not all of the cards in a sequence will come into play. If, for example, the 8 of diamonds is in the dummy hand, the player who put down the last card (i.e. the 7 of diamonds) must start another sequence by putting down the lowest black card (black, because the last sequence was red) in his hand.

Then play continues by building up in that suit. Players put down whatever cards they can. In most games,

each suit will come into play on more than one occasion. When starting a new sequence, players should choose the suit in which they hold most cards, in order to empty their hands more quickly.

If a player has to start a sequence in one colour, but only has cards of the other left in his hand, he has to 'pass' and play moves to the player on his left to start a sequence in the required colour. When a player puts down a 'horse' card in the sequence, he can collect all the chips or matchsticks that were bet on that horse. Players must pick up their winnings quickly – if another player puts down the next card in the sequence before the winnings are collected, then it is too late and the chips or

matchsticks must stay on that horse until the next round, thus increasing the stakes to be won.

When one player gets rid of all his cards, he collects all the chips or matchsticks in the kitty as a reward for crossing the finishing line first, and the round comes to an end. At the start of the game, players decide how many rounds they are going to play.

If a player runs out of matches, either he has to stand down, or a wealthier player may decide to loan him some chips or matches to continue, attaching conditions if they are feeling ruthless! Once all the rounds have been played, the person who has managed to collect the most chips or matchsticks is the overall winner.

Newmarket

Sample hands

This player holds one horse card.
He decides to stick with his hand.

This player doesn't hold any horse cards: he decides to swap his hand
for the dummy. Fortunately the dummy contains the ace of clubs.

This player holds two horse cards – an excellent hand.

The horse cards

Games for Three or More Players

Three is a significant number in
cards, as it is in many aspects of
life. It is the minimum number
necessary to enable players
to combine in an alliance.
Below is a selection of games
that require between three
and six players.

Black Maria

Number of players
From three to six.

Aim of game
By gaining tricks without winning any cards from the hearts suit, or the queen of spades (Black Maria).

Method of play
Use the standard pack of 52. With three players, take out the 2 of clubs. Always make sure that equal numbers of cards are dealt. Aces are high.

Cut for dealer (lowest card). Dealing goes to the left. All the cards are dealt out, one at a time. Once a player has seen his hand, he can place any three cards face down, to be picked up by the player on his left; and he must pick up three from the player on his right.

The opening lead is made by the player on the dealer's left. Other players must follow suit if they can; otherwise

Each player will have 13 cards each with four players.

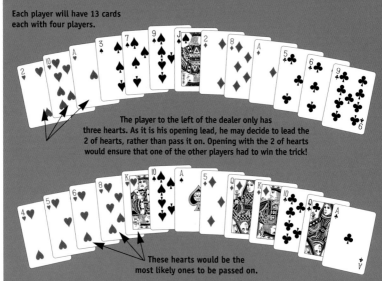

The player to the left of the dealer only has three hearts. As it is his opening lead, he may decide to lead the 2 of hearts, rather than pass it on. Opening with the 2 of hearts would ensure that one of the other players had to win the trick!

These hearts would be the most likely ones to be passed on.

Black Maria

any card may be played. There are no trumps. The highest card of the leading suit wins. The winning player leads to the next trick. After each hand, the deal moves to the next player on the left.

The aim is to avoid winning tricks that contain hearts or Black Maria, the queen of spades.

Scoring

At the end of each round, all the players add up their scores of hearts. Each heart card won counts for one point.

Before the game players agree a score that will end the game – usually 50. Play continues until one player reaches this score. The player with the lowest score is the winner.

Penalty card

The queen of spades is treated as an additional heart, but counting for 20 points.

Bonus card

The jack of diamonds can be treated as a bonus card, allowing a deduction of 10 points.

This player doesn't have many hearts in his hand after the deal.

The dealer has two hearts and the queen of spades.

Brag

The most common form of Brag is Three-Card Brag.

Number of players
Three to six.

Aim of game
To win the pool by ending with the strongest hand.

Method of play

Use a 52-card pack. Aces are high, except for ace, 2, 3 – when they are low. Stake limits are agreed at the start and cards are cut to find the dealer (highest card, with ace high).

Dealer sets the agreed stake and deals three cards, one at a time, face down, to each player. The remainder go face up to his left.

Eldest hand is first to bet, and may do so without looking at his cards. If he looks, he can then bet (holding his hand) or drop out, in which case he places his cards on top of the stock. If he bets blind, he does not touch his cards. The turn passes to the player on the left, who has the same choice of betting

blind or open. If he bets blind and the previous bet was also blind, it must be an amount equal to or greater than the previous bet. If he is betting 'open' and the previous bet was blind, then he must bet at least double the previous one. If he bets blind and the one before him was open, he need only bet half. In a later round, a player may switch from betting blind to betting open. If he then decides to drop out, his cards go on the stock and his stake is lost. A player betting the same amount as the previous bet says 'stay' and names the sum. A player increasing the bet says 'raise' and names the sum.

Play continues until only two players remain

in play. If both are playing open, either may call to see the other's hand, so long as he is at least matching the other's previous stake. On seeing the other hand, the caller may then drop out, without showing his own hand, and lose; or show that he has a better hand, and win. If one player is betting blind and the other is betting open, then the player betting open must continue to double the blind player's stake, or drop out. If both are betting blind, play continues until one does look at his cards. However, it is possible for one blind player to call another; but not for an open player to call a blind one. The winner takes the pool.

Brag

Scoring

Prial: Three of the same rank, e.g. 2-2-2.

Flush Run: Three in suit and sequence, e.g. 2-3-4 of hearts.

Run: Any three in sequence, e.g. 2-3-4 of mixed suits.

Flush: Any three in the same suit.

High card: No combination, but highest card, or second or third if there is a tie, wins.

Pair: Two of same rank plus a singleton, e.g. 2-2-9.

In Pairs, a higher pair beats a lower pair, and equal pairs are decided by the singleton. Some players take a prial of 3-3-3 as beating any other; and also ace-2-3 as beating queen-king-ace.

Variant
American Brag

In this version, jacks and 9s are braggers. These are all equal in value, and the highest hand is a hand of three braggers. A combination including a bragger outranks a natural hand of the same value. American Brag is more likely to end in a tie, in which case the pool is divided evenly.

In American Brag the highest hand is three jacks.

Poker

There are two basic forms of Poker, Draw and Stud Poker, and each has many variants. However, there are certain standard features, and once you know these, it is easy to join in any adaptation of the game.

Number of players
Three or more. Five to eight is best for Draw Poker, seven to ten for Stud Poker.

Aim of game
By having the highest-ranking hand at the end of the game.

Method of play
Use the standard 52-card pack. Aces can be high or low. The suits are all of equal value.

Draw Poker
To choose the dealer, any player distributes cards from a shuffled pack; first to get a jack becomes the first dealer.

The cards are shuffled three times, lastly by the dealer, and the player to dealer's right cuts.

Cards are dealt one at a time, from the dealer's left, until each player has five cards.

Scoring
All poker hands consist of five cards. Depending on your hand, you score it as follows (highest to lowest):

Straight flush: Five cards in suit and sequence, with ace being either high or low. A Royal Flush (ace-high, king, queen, jack, ten straight flush) beats any other.

Four of a kind: Four cards of the same value (e.g. four queens or four 4s), plus any other card. A higher-ranking set beats a lower-ranking one.

Full house: Three of one kind and a pair of another kind (e.g. three queens and two 4s). A higher-ranking set beats a lower-ranking one (e.g. four 3s and a queen beat four 2s and a king).

Poker

Flush: Five cards all of the same suit, but not making up a complete sequence. If two players have flushes, the one with the higher top card wins. If the top cards match, then highest second card wins, and so on.

Straight: Five cards in complete sequence of rank, with ace either high or low, but of different suits. Higher top card beats a lower one.

Three of a kind: Three cards of the same value, plus two others which are not a pair. A higher-ranking set beats a lower-ranking one.

Two pairs: Two sets of two of the same value, plus any other card. Highest ranks win if two players have two pairs.

One pair: Two cards of the same value, the others all singletons. Highest ranked pair or highest singleton wins.

Poker

Betting

Stakes should be agreed in advance (cash or chips). Each player places a chip in the pool at the start. One player acts as banker.

Betting normally starts to the dealer's left and goes clockwise. In some schools, no player is allowed to open the betting unless he holds a pair of jacks or a higher combination.

You can either call, raise or fold (sometimes called drop). If you fold, you discard your hand and lose your stake. If you call, you must put into the pool enough chips to match, but not exceed, what any other player has bet in that round. If you raise, you add more value to the call amount, subject to an agreed upper limit.

When you raise, you must say clearly the amount you are raising the bet by.

Once everyone has made a bet, or folded, the players still in the game may discard up to three cards, and receive replacement cards from the dealer. Another betting round follows and the players again call, raise or fold. Previous bets cannot be withdrawn.

At the end of each betting round, each player has to have put the same amount into the pool. Any player who does not do so, must fold.

The Showdown: This is when hands are shown. The highest hand (see Scoring) wins the pot.

Stud Poker

Arrangements for agreeing stakes and choosing dealer are the same as for Draw Poker.

Five-Card Stud

The dealer deals a round of cards face down (the 'hole-card'), then a round of cards face up. Each player looks at his own hole-card. The player with the highest face-up card (nearest the dealer if there is a tie) either bets or folds. Other players in sequence from the left call, raise or fold. Another upcard is then dealt to each player still in the game, beginning with the player with the top pair of upcards, and another round of betting begins. A third upcard is dealt to the surviving players, and the player with the three best upcards opens the betting. Finally, a fourth upcard is dealt, and the round of betting is done on the same basis as before. After the final call, all hole-cards are turned over to expose each player's whole hand.

Poker

Hole-card

One pair

Flush

Hole-card

Hole-card

Three of a kind

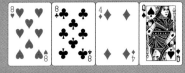

Two pairs

In Five-Card Stud the hole-cards are not turned over until after the final round of betting.

Hole-card

Poker

Six-Card Stud

In this version there is an additional second face-down hole-card, dealt at the end. But only five cards are produced for the showdown, leaving the player to decide which card to eliminate.

Whisky Poker

The players agree the stake to be paid into the pool. The dealer is chosen as for standard poker. The dealer deals five cards to each player, with an extra hand, the 'widow', dealt face down on the table. Eldest hand starts play, and he can choose to take up the widow and replace it with his own hand, face up, or refuse it. If he refuses, the choice passes to his left. If every player refuses the widow, then the dealer spreads it face up on the table. Now, starting again with eldest hand, a player can pick up the whole widow, or draw just one card from it, replacing it either with his own hand or one card from his hand, or stand (decline to draw). Once he has done so, or stood, the turn passes to his left, and so on until one player knocks on the table to signify he is happy with his hand.

The other players now have one more chance each, to draw or to stand. There are no bets or raises within the game, and it now goes straight to the showdown, in which each player shows his hand. Scoring the hands is as for standard poker, and the winner takes the pool.

Wild Cards: Introducing Wild Cards, either by having a joker, or naming the deuce (2) as wild, extends the range of possibilities. Five of a kind now becomes top scorer, with four aces plus the Wild Card beating any other combination.

High Card: Any hand which is not one of those shown on pages 38–9. Highest value wins. If nobody has a pair or better, then the highest card wins. If there is a tie for highest, then the next highest wins, and so on.

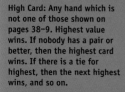

Wild Card

Poker

Sample hands in Whisky Poker

There are no cards in the widow which will help this player!

Three of a kind

This is the best hand the player can obtain.

One pair

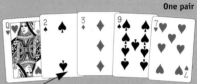

By swapping one of his cards, this player can get one pair.

Widow

Flush

This player cannot improve his hand.

Full house

This player can get a full house by swapping his 2 of diamonds for the 4 of spades.

43

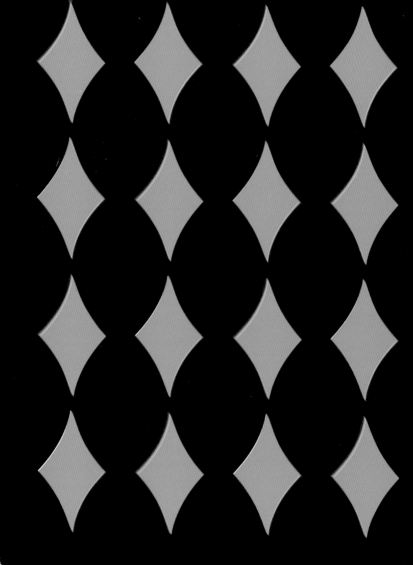

44

Games for Four or More Players

You need four people to play the classic versions of some of the best-known games, such as Whist and Bridge, which involve two sets of partners playing against each other. This can be very exciting – you are trying to read your partner's mind and guess what is in his hand, and you could have a shared bet at stake if you are playing for money. This section will also look at Blackjack and Solo, which can be played by four or more players.

Blackjack

This gambling game is the American form of Pontoon (see pages 22–25).

Number of players
Four to six is best.

Aim of game
By reaching a total of 21, or as close as possible beneath it.

Card values
Ace is 1 or 11; king, queen, jack all 10; other cards by pip value.

Method of play
Use the standard 52-card pack. Aces can be high or low. Players should agree the maximum stake before play begins. Cut or draw for dealer (lowest card). Dealer then deals a single card to each player, including himself. Having seen his card, each player places a bet on it (the ante), up to the agreed maximum. The banker does not bet, but may double: if he does, any player unwilling to go double loses his stake. Players may also redouble.

The banker then deals a second card all round. Any player then holding an ace (11) or a court card or a 10 (ten) has a 'natural 21' and the banker pays him double his stake, unless the banker also has a natural. In that case, the banker collects the player's stake, plus double the stake of any player who does not hold a natural.

If no player has a natural, the banker deals further cards, face up, as the player calls for them. The aim is to get to 21 or as near as possible, without going over (bust). The player can call 'stand' when he wants to stop, or say 'twist', or 'hit me' if he wants to continue receiving cards.

If the player is bust, the banker gets his stake. Players who have chosen to stand, wait until the banker has dealt further cards to himself. If the banker goes bust, he pays the stake back to each standing player. If the dealer too stands, then each player shows his full hand. The dealer pays off players with a total higher than his own (but less than 22) and collects from any with a lesser or the same total as himself.

Blackjack

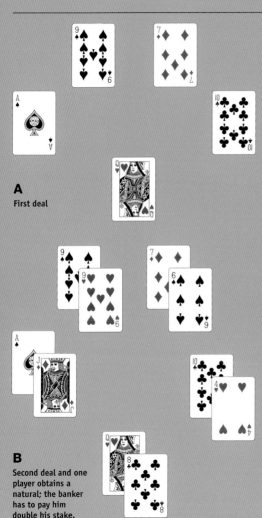

A
First deal

B
Second deal and one player obtains a natural; the banker has to pay him double his stake.

Splitting

If a player's first two cards are of the same number value, he can split them into two hands, on which he can draw, or stand. He must bet equally on each split hand. Cards must also be of equal rank to be split (i.e. two kings may be split, but not a king and a 10).

Doubling down

If a player's first two cards total 11, he can turn both cards face up, while doubling his bet and receiving a third card. He must then stand on these three cards and can only look at the third card when all other players have played their hands.

The deal stays with the original banker, but he can sell the bank to the highest bidder before or after any hand. If a player has a natural (and the banker doesn't), he takes over the bank in the next hand. If more than one player has a natural, the deal goes to the one nearest the banker's left.

Games for Four or More Players

Bridge

Also called Contract Bridge, this is perhaps the most widely played card game in the world. It is a demanding game, but, rather like chess, it can be enjoyed at any level by opponents who are more or less evenly matched.

Number of players
Four, playing as two partnerships.

Aim of game
By being the first side to win two games.

Method of play
Use the standard 52-card pack. Aces are high. It is usual to have a second pack, shuffled, ready for the next dealer. Players sit with partners facing each other: North-South; East-West. Cut or draw for dealer. Before each deal, the pack is cut by the player to the dealer's right. The dealer then deals 13 cards, one at a time, to each player.

Bidding
Also known as the Auction, this starts with the dealer, who bids for the number of tricks he expects himself and his partner to take. He also specifies the trump suit,

or states, 'no trump'. Scoring only begins after six tricks have been won, and the lowest bid is one (i.e. seven tricks). For example, 'four spades' means he expects to score 10 tricks with spades as trumps.

Bids run in ascending order: clubs, diamonds (the minor suits) hearts, spades (major suits), and no trumps. The lowest bid is therefore one club, and the highest is seven no trumps. Alternatively, a bidder can 'pass' or 'no bid' (no tricks over six). Bidding then moves to the left.

If all players pass, hands are turned in and the deal moves to the

left. If a bid is made, the next player can raise it (e.g. from one spade to two spades) or go higher (e.g. one heart over one diamond). A player may double a bid made by the opposing team. This means that if the bid is reached, they score double trick points; if they fail, the opposing side gets the trick points. The next player to call can overcall (make a higher bid) or redouble the already-doubled bid, which redoubles the potential gain for either side. Note that players do not double or redouble their own partner's bids. Players may re-bid, but when three have

48

Bridge

Sample Bridge hands

This hand is worth 10 points (see page 51).

A

Bid: Despite the low point-count, the long suit is worth opening at One Heart (your partner has a one-in-three chance of holding the ace).

This hand is worth 13 points (see page 51).

B

Bid: Open at One Spade and see if your partner has strength, perhaps in diamonds.

49

Bridge

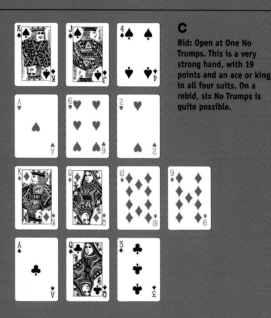

C

Bid: Open at One No Trumps. This is a very strong hand, with 19 points and an ace or king in all four suits. On a rebid, six No Trumps is quite possible.

the last to bid becomes the Declarer, and plays the hand for the bidding team, unless he names the same trump suit (or no trumps) as his partner did, in which case the partner becomes Declarer. Players on the declaring side must win at least as many tricks as they bid; the defending side tries to prevent them.

Play begins with the opponent on the Declarer's left. The usual lead for this player would be the highest card of the suit his partner called. If the partner did not bid, then the player should lead with the fourth highest of his longest and strongest suit The Declarer's partner then lays his hand face up

on the table, arranging it in suits, in descending order from the aces. This enables the Declarer to play it as a 'dummy' hand while also playing his own hand; his partner cannot assist in any way. Play goes to the left; players must follow suit if they can; otherwise they may either trump or play a

Bridge

discard. Highest card of the suit led, or highest trump, takes the trick. The The winner of the trick leads to the next, and so on until all 13 tricks have been taken.

Scoring

Tricks are scored in ascending value, according to the trump suit, or 'no trumps.' In clubs and diamonds, each trick scored (after the first six) counts as 20 points. In hearts and spades, each trick scored counts as 30 points. With 'no trumps', the first trick scored is at 40 points, with 30 points for each additional trick. If the bid has been doubled, the scores are doubled, and multiplied by four if redoubled.

The first side to score 100 trick points wins, and play resumes in a fresh game. The rubber ends if the same team wins two games in a row; otherwise it is the best of three.

Scoring method

To ensure accuracy, both sides keep the score for the other side as well as for themselves. A special printed sheet is usually employed, or can be drawn up, with a column for each side (headed US and THEM), and a horizontal line marked across the middle.

Trick points (including doubles) are entered below this line, and bonus points above it. Bonus points are awarded for tricks won over and above the contract; for winning a contract to take 12 tricks (Small Slam) or 13 tricks (Grand Slam); and for defeating a contract. Bonus points are also awarded to players who happen to get the honour cards (ace down to 10) of the trump suit, or all four aces if the call is 'no trumps.' This applies to each individual's hand, not to the combined hands of the partnership.

The side to win the first game of a rubber is then called 'vulnerable' and different scoring rates apply to it (see table on page 52).

Conventions

Effective bridge play means that the players in the two partnerships must use the same 'language': during the auction they cannot see each other's hands and have to rely on applying the same bidding pattern to get an understanding of what each is holding.

Numerous systems have been devised to achieve this, One of the most straightforward is to assign points to individual cards, once your hand is sorted into suits, in descending order of value from left to right.

The ace, king queen and jack are known as 'Honours' (or high-point) cards, and are worth the following points: ace 4; king 3; queen 2; jack 1.

Bridge

Scoring Table for Contract Bridge

Declarer's side, below the line score

For each odd
odd trick over six

	Ordinary Contract	Doubled	Redoubled
Minor suits	20	40	80
Major suits	30	60	120
No trump: first trick	40	80	120
Further tricks	30	60	120

Declarer's side, above the line score

	Not vulnerable Minor, Major & NT		Vulnerable Minor Major & NT		Making Contract
Each overtrick	20	30	20	30	No bonus
When doubled	100	100	200	200	50
When redoubled	200	200	400	400	50
Small Slam	500	500	750	750	
Grand Slam	1000	1000	1500	1500	

Defenders' above the line score when declarers fail to make contract

	Not vulnerable All suits & NT	Vulnerable All suits & NT
Each undertrick	50	100
Doubled: first undertrick	100	200
Each further undertrick	200	400
Redoubled: first undertrick	200	400
Each further undertrick	400	600

US	THEM	US	THEM

Winners' bonus points (above the line)

Win rubber in 2 games	Rubber in 2 out of 3	One game, rubber unfinished	Part score, game unfinished
700	500	300	50

Bonus points for Honour Cards held

Trump suit 4 in one hand	No trumps 5 in one hand	(All the Aces) All in one hand
100	150	150

Bridge

Normally a Bridge partnership will have a combined strength of around 20. With 25 in high cards you should win the game; with 37 you should achieve a Grand Slam. If your high cards come to less than 13, leave the opening bid to your partner, unless you have five or more of a suit to an honour card (see hand A, page 49).

Four or more cards of the same suit in your hand make a long suit; three or less a short suit. Count an extra point for any fourth or more card in a side (non-trump) suit, and any fifth or more card in a trump suit. To open with a suit bid of one (naming trumps) you should hold 12 to 14 points in that suit. With two biddable suits, bid the longer; if they are of equal length, bid the higher-scoring one. For a trump bid of two, you need at least seven cards in your trump suit and a value of 19. This is a very strong signal to your partner.

The most common opening bid is one trick, and the partner's responding bid must convey a message back about the strength of his own hand, which will then determine what happens in the next round of bidding. He can raise in the same suit, make a higher bid in a new suit, or bid no trumps. If he has at least three cards of the first bidder's named trump suit, he can safely raise the bid to two.

Cautious bidding should be the rule until players have got a feeling for the game, and developed an understanding with their partner. It is a good idea to practise bidding patterns outside the framework of an actual game.

Bridge terms

Acol system
Named after Acol Street, London, where this bidding system was worked out in 1934, it is now the standard for British tournament play. Like the SAYC system used in the USA, Canada and Australia, it's not for beginners, but you can pick up a lot of useful information from an Acol handbook.

Average hand
A hand with 10 high-card points.

Forcing bid
A very strong bid that requires your partner to keep the bidding going, i.e. not to pass if the intervening player passes.

Forcing lead
If you are leader and hold, say, four cards of the trump suit, you lead the way aimed at weakening the Declarer's trump suit by forcing him to play trumps.

Bridge

North

West

East

South

1 Establishing a suit

As South and Declarer, you have a long suit in diamonds and should get at least three tricks from your ace, king, queen. However, you don't know whether East or West holds the other five diamonds. In Bridge, probabilities guide your decisions on play. The probability is that one holds three and the other holds two. Play to this probability, first taking tricks with your ace, king and queen, and cleaning out the opposing team's diamonds. Then you have two safe tricks with your 7 and 2. You may be wrong, but you are more likely to be right.

2 Calculating probabilities

‣ If you hold eight cards, then the opponents' five is most likely to break 3–2.
‣ If you hold seven cards, then the opponents' six is most likely to break 4–2 (not 3–3 as you might suppose)
‣ If you hold six cards of a suit, then the

Bridge

Bridge hints 3

North

West

East

South

opponents' seven is most likely to break 4–3.

❧ If you hold five cards of a suit, the opponents' eight is most likely to break 5–3.

3 The finesse

Again, this is a matter of weighing up the probabilities. Playing as Declarer, you try to get the opposition to play its high card before you play your high card.

Playing from South, you don't know that West holds the king. The chance is 50:50 between West and East. Your best tactic is to lead with the queen. If West then plays the king, you beat it with the ace.

If West plays a lower card, you play a low card from Dummy and wait for East, knowing that if he

does not play the king you can't lose the trick.

If East had the king, you would lose that trick, but the others would be safely yours.

Key hint for finessing

You need to have the card above and below the one you are finessing (in this case ace and queen to finesse the king).

Solo

Number of players
Four.

Aim of game
The highest bidder plays against the other three to take the number of tricks he bid for at the start of the game

Method of play
Use a standard 52-card pack. Aces are high. Cut for dealer.

Starting from his left, the dealer deals 13 cards to each player, in four batches of three and a one. The dealer turns over the final card and lays it on the table to propose the trump suit. He takes it into his hand when an 'auction' (bidding) has been completed.

Bidding
Bids (or calls) are made by each player in turn, starting with the player on the dealer's left.

Players can make a higher bid, or pass, or accept a proposal. A player who has passed once may not bid again.

If a bid is followed by three consecutive passes, the bidder is the soloist.

Possible bids in ascending order

Proposal: a player says 'I propose,' or 'prop', if he thinks he and another player can take at least eight tricks using the proposed trump suit.

Cop: the acceptance of a 'prop'. It can only be made after a prop and provided no other player has made a stronger call. If no further bid is made, this bid stands and the two play as partners for the round.

Solo: a bid to take at least five tricks using the proposed trump suit.

Misere: a bid to take no tricks. If this bid is made the trump suit is

cancelled and the hand is played without a trump suit

Abundance: a bid to win nine or more tricks using a trump suit named by the bidder.

Royal Abundance: a bid to win at least nine tricks using the proposed trump suit.

Spread Misere: a bid to win no tricks, again playing without a trump suit. The caller must lead the first card and play the hand with his cards exposed face up on the table.

Abundance Declared: a bid to win all 13 tricks, without a trump suit. The caller must lead the first card. This is the highest bid of all.

Solo

If the eldest hand proposes and all other players pass, he is able to raise his call to a solo. If eldest hand passes, and another player proposes, without any higher call being made, eldest hand has the option of accepting the proposal.

If all pass, the cards are thrown in and the deal passes to the left. If a player calls 'prop' and none of the other three players call 'cop' or make a call of greater strength, the situation is the same as if they had all passed and a new deal begins.

Once the contract is made, the dealer takes the turned-up card into his hand and eldest hand leads, except in the case of Abundance Declared (unless he is also the soloist). Tricks are taken in the normal way: the highest card

of a suit or the highest trump wins. Players must follow suit if possible; and the winner of the trick leads to the next.

Scoring

If the soloist makes his contract, he receives points from the other players; otherwise he pays points:

Proposal and acceptance	2
Solo	2
Misere	3
Abundance (including royal):	4
Spread Misere	6
Abundance Declared	8

In the case of proposal/acceptance, each of the partners receives or pays.

For each trick under or over the amount bid, a point is paid by the bidder, or by each of his opponents.

If a Misere bidder takes a trick, or an Abundance Declared bidder loses one, all hands are abandoned and points counted immediately.

Variant
Three-handed Solo

To play this game, remove all 2s, 3s and 4s from a standard pack, making a 40-card pack.

Each player receives 13 cards and the 40th card is turned face up to show trumps.

The proposal system of bidding is not employed; it is each player for himself.

Bidding and scoring are the same as in the four-handed version.

Games for Four or More Players

Solo

A good Solo hand
Proposed trump suit: hearts

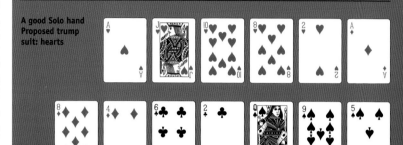

Solo should be a safe bid. If someone has already bid Solo you might try Royal abundance, though that would be pushing it without more court cards in the non-trump suits.

A better Solo hand
Proposed trump suit: diamonds

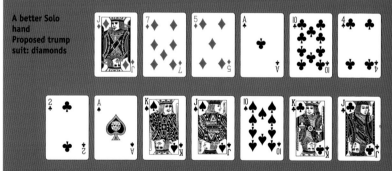

Abundance in spades is a possible bid, though one more lower spade would have made it more secure.

Solo

A Misere hand.
Proposed trump suit: spades

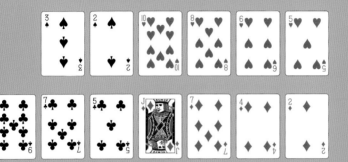

If hearts were trumps, a proposal would be possible, but misere brings
a higher score. Take care with your higher cards though. Remember
that all the other players will be trying to force you to win.

Whist

This is one of the most popular partnership games. Its relative simplicity makes it a good game to play with a partner picked at random.

Number of players
Four, playing as two sets of partners.

Aim of game
By taking more tricks than the opposing partnership, to win two games out of three.

Method of play
Use the standard pack of 52. It is usual to use two packs, with different back designs, so that one may be shuffled while the other is being dealt. Aces are high.

Players draw cards to decide partners, who sit facing each other across the table. The draw can be decided according to either suit or value. A draw is also made to find the dealer (highest card, with aces low).

The dealer deals out 13 cards to each player, one at a time, starting with the player to his left. The last card is turned face up to determine trumps: the dealer then adds it to his hand.

The player to the dealer's left leads to the first trick. Others must follow suit if they can, otherwise trump or discard. The highest card of the led suit or a trump card wins. The normal lead is the fourth card in your longest non-trump suit.

One partner for each team takes charge of the tricks it has won. The winner of a trick leads to the next trick.

Scoring
A partnership has to take at least seven tricks to score. The first six tricks won have no scoring value. After the seventh, each trick counts for one point. Revoking is penalized by

three points. The first side to gain five points wins the game.

Points are also given for honour cards held. If a team receive the ace, king, queen and jack of the trump suit (honour cards), they gain an extra four points. If they receive any three of the honour cards, they gain an extra two points. Points for honour cards are only given to a side which starts the deal with a score of less than four points.

Winning
Whist is normally played in a set of three games (this is called a Rubber). The first side to win two games out of three wins the Rubber.

Whist

A typical game: spades are trumps, with the ace of spades having been taken up by the dealer (South). This is the position after the first nine hands have been played, with five tricks to North-South and four to East-West.

North

West

East

South

Hand 10
South leads JC
West plays JS (Why not his 5S? It's a gamble on North having no clubs and no court spades.)
North plays 2C
East plays 9H

Hand 11
West leads 4D (would have done better with unbeatable KS, knowing the QS is still in play).
North plays 10S
East plays 4S
South plays 10H

Hand 12
North leads QS
East plays 7S
South plays 2S
West plays KS

Hand 13
West leads 5S
North plays 6C
East plays 9S
South plays 10C

The final result is seven tricks to East-West and six to North-South. With more than half the trump suit, East-West should have done better. Perhaps trying to be too clever, East made a mistake at hand 10, when the 5S should have been played, leaving the king and jack available to win later tricks. East also went wrong at hand 11, when he should have won the trick with KS.

Glossary of Terms

Ace high: Ace is top scoring card.

Ace low: Ace is lowest scoring card.

Ante: Also known as the stake. The amount each player pays into the pool at the start of a gambling game.

Available card: In Patience, a card that can be used in play.

Build up: In Patience, laying cards in ascending order of value on top of a foundation card.

Build down: Laying the cards in descending order of value.

Chips: Tokens used in gambling games.

Column: Cards laid on the table in an overlapping vertical line.

Court cards: Kings, queens and jacks.

Deal: Passing out cards to players. Most deals are one card at a time to each player, but this can vary according to the game.

Deck: American term for the pack.

Discard: Either to play a card of no value in the game, when the player cannot follow suit or play a trump; or to play a card to the waste pile.

Eldest hand: The player on the dealer's left, who normally leads.

File: In Patience, a column in the layout, with cards overlapping but with suits and pip values visible. Files are built up towards the player.

Flush: A hand of cards all of the same suit.

Follow suit: To play a card of the same suit as the first card played in a trick.

Foundation card: In Patience, a card laid down on which other cards are built up or down. They are usually aces or kings.

Hand: The cards held by a player at any point during the game. In Patience, it can also be any cards which have not been dealt out (also called the stock).

Honour cards: Ace, king, queen and jack of the trump suit.

Layout: The arrangement of cards in Patience games. Also called the tableau.

Kitty: See Pool.

Lead: Being first player to set down a card. Also the card played first (lead card).

Meld: a set, usually of three or more of a kind; e.g. either all kings, or all hearts (but these must be in sequence of pip value with no gaps).

Number card: Card of any value between 10 and 2.

Pack: The full set of 52 cards (or 53 with a joker). Also known as a deck.

Packet: Set of cards that is less than a full pack.

Pair: Two cards of the same kind, e.g. two 2s.

Pass: To miss a turn.

Glossary of Terms

Patience: A range of card games in which a single player can play against the pack. Also called Solitaire.

Pip value: The number on a number card (e.g. a nine has nine pips). The value of court cards varies from game to game.

Pool: Total amount of cash or gambling chips staked in a game, usually placed in the middle of the table. Also called the kitty, or the pot.

Plain card: Card not of the trump suit.

Play: To play a card is to take it from your hand and use it in the game.

Rank: The value of a card.

Redeal: In Patience, using the cards from the waste pile to deal again, when the stock is used up.

Renege: To fail to follow suit in a game where following suit is not obligatory. Often confused with Revoke.

Revoke: To play an incorrect card, e.g. by failing to follow suit when able to; in a game where following suit is obligatory if you can do so. Often confused with Renege.

Round: This is complete once each player has played his cards in any trick.

Row: In Patience, a line of cards placed side by side (suit and pip value must always be visible if cards overlap).

Rubber: A set of games, especially in Whist.

Ruff: A trump card. To ruff is to play a trump to a non-trump lead.

School: A group of players playing for money, especially in Poker.

Sequence: The order in which the cards run, from high to low, or the other way round.

Singleton: A single card of any suit.

Stock: The cards remaining after dealing, sometimes also called the hand.

Tableau: Another word for layout, in Patience games.

Talon: Another word for waste pile, in Patience.

Trick: The cards played by all the players in a round, one from each.

Trumps: A chosen suit that outranks all cards in all other suits during the game. To trump is to play a trump card.

Upcard: A card dealt face up for all to see.

Waste pile: Cards turned up in the course of playing Patience that are not available for play according to the rules of the game. Also sometimes called the talon.

Wild Card: A card which a player can use to represent any other card (within the rules of the game).

Index